Rosa Vertner Jeffrey

Daisy Dare, and Baby Power

Poems

Rosa Vertner Jeffrey

Daisy Dare, and Baby Power
Poems

ISBN/EAN: 9783337042349

Printed in Europe, USA, Canada, Australia, Japan

Cover: Foto ©Thomas Meinert / pixelio.de

More available books at **www.hansebooks.com**

DAISY DARE.

DAISY DARE,

AND

BABY POWER:

POEMS.

BY
ROSA VERTNER JEFFREY.

With Eight Illustrations,
Designed by D. Vertner Johnson, Esq.

PHILADELPHIA:
CLAXTON, REMSEN & HAFFELFINGER,
819 AND 821 MARKET STREET.
1871.

Entered according to Act of Congress, in the year 1870, by
ROSA VERTNER JEFFREY,
in the Office of the Librarian of Congress at Washington.

STEREOTYPED BY J. FAGAN & SON.   PRINTED BY MOORE BROS.

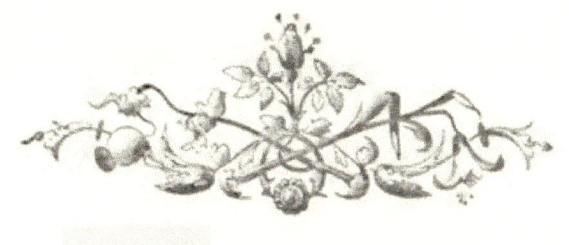

TO

MY DEAR FRIEND

MRS. MARGARET WICKLIFFE PRESTON,

OF LEXINGTON, KENTUCKY,

THIS VOLUME IS

Affectionately Inscribed

BY THE AUTHOR.

LEXINGTON, KY., December 1, 1870.

"At early morn swept Daisy Dare,—
Sparkling, graceful, passing fair."

DAISY DARE.

PART I.

THRO' scented meadows, where do graze
  The meek-eyed kine on summer days,
At early morn swept Daisy Dare,—
Sparkling, graceful, passing fair.

Sparkling as the dew-drops gleaming
On her path, or sunlight streaming
Through her tresses—graceful, fair,
As naught on earth save Daisy Dare!

Wondrous tresses! sunshine fades
Mid floating curls and sumptuous braids,—
A crown of light that glorifies
White brow and deep impassioned eyes.

Full, perfect, tempting were her lips—
The bee or humming-bird that sips
From scarlet blossoms in the South
Beguiled might be by such a mouth.

Her path ran by a rushing stream
Which, like a crooked silver seam,
Bound that green meadow to a wood,
Where soon with Graham Lee she stood.

Softly through arching forest-trees
Came stealing up a fresh salt breeze;
One fair cheek kissing, till it burned
Like to the other Lee-ward turned.

"Daisy," he said, "I sail to-day
For India, with Captain Gray;
Will you not be upon the strand
To say 'farewell'— to wave your hand?"

"Yes; I will go to see you sail:"
The tone was proud — her cheek turned pale;
"I've promised to be there and say
A parting word to Allen Gray."

The strong man's cheek grew white as death
As thus, with short, unsteady breath,
He said: "When last I went to sea,
You waved, nay, kissed your hand to me."

Her eyes flashed, smiling on him then —
Such eyes hold fiery, earnest men
In bondage, and to love beguile,
Whether they mock, or weep, or smile.

"Yes; I remember then to you
I kissed my hand; but here are two:
Can I not still kiss this one, pray,
To you, and this to Allen Gray?"

"Oh, do not mock me, Daisy Dare,
 With your small hands so soft and fair."

Her voice was deep, the words were light,
The hands upheld were small and white, —
Such hands as strong men love to grasp
And crush in an impassioned clasp.

"Oh, do not mock me, Daisy Dare,
With your small hands so soft and fair;
They may beguile both lovers — true;
You cannot give your heart to two.

"One or the other let it be;
If Allen Gray, you're lost to me:
If me, all hearts you must resign, —
All homage and all love save mine.

"My guiding star across the brine,
Has been the hope that called you mine;
I'd rather see that load-star set,
Than wed a fair, false, vain coquette.

"I'd rather trust, though seas divide,
Than linger doubting by your side:
Now speak, what turns your heart away;
The love of gold or Allen Gray?"

Up rose her spirit, quick and proud;
And, as through a translucent cloud
Pour crimson streams of torrid light,
The red blood dyed her forehead white.

DAISY DARE.

"I have not broken faith or vow,"
She said; "but do release you now.
My heart cannot be bought or sold
By Allen Gray with love or gold.

"I trifled with him but to try
Your faith in me: I'd rather die
Than wed a man of jealous heart:
You cannot trust me, let us part.

"The jealous love you bring to me,
(As yonder green, impulsive sea
Unto the shore doth come and go,)
In passion tides would ebb and flow.

"And as that surf, in fitful swells,
Doth bring or bear away the shells
From yonder strand, — such passion, strife
Would fill, or desolate my life.

"Such earthly crown of love to wear,
The cross it brings I would not bear;
Here! see me cast the burden down:
Go! — for I yield you up the crown."

The angry flush had faded now,
Leaving her bosom, cheek, and brow
Whiter than sea-foam 'neath the moon;
Her low voice as sad wind-harp's tune.

DAISY DARE.

She waved her hand and turned away:
He caught it, crying, "Daisy, stay!
Let not a flash of passion-pride
Two clinging hearts like ours divide."

She stood before him haughty, cold:
"You taunted me with love of gold—
Who wealth and titles scorned—to be
The chosen bride of Graham Lee."

"This choice, perhaps, you now regret,
And crave a titled suitor yet;
Hearts that are anchored side by side,
No surface-ripple can divide."

His words were bitter in their turn,
And, like sharp acid on a burn,
They scorched her heart, and seared the spot
Where blossomed love's "forget-me-not."

Oh, why are darts of anger hurled
From heart to heart throughout the world;
Fierce as the lightning — flashing far,
From cloud to cloud, its red-hot bar?

So quick, so sharp, too oft it cleaves
The sandal-chain of love, and leaves
But fragrant, broken, links at last
To bind us to a ruined past.

Too often fixing deeps of woe
Between us and the long ago;
Bridging a gulf toward mem'ries green,
With one regret — "it might have been."

Oh, why, when life is in its June
Of fruity fragrance, perfect tune,
Does passion's stormy pride destroy
Youths' heritage of love and joy?

One jealous breath will oft disclose
A canker in hope's perfect rose,
For the false fever heat of strife
To nurse, and nourish into life.

Oh, Daisy Dare! the sea is wide:
Dear is the lover by thy side:
The sea is treacherous, hungry, deep,
And millions o'er its treasures weep.

His heart relented — strong hearts do;
Yet more relenting, oft less true
Than those, unyielding, that defy
The deathless love of which they die.

"As forest saplings, by the sun
Together knit till two are one —
One trunk, one bark, one sap, one tree —
Our hearts have been, should ever be.

"Let sharp steel cleave that circling rind,
No art its severed strength could bind;
Should anger part thy love from mine,
Holds earth another heart for thine?"

Oh, stubborn pride! unyielding still;
Her heart is conquered; but her will
Defies its tender, pleading tone:
She left him — they were both alone.

* * * * * * * * * * * *

When eve her golden goblet fills
Among the sunset's purple hills,
And overflows that sunset wine
In streams of glory on the brine,

Unto the shore a maiden came,
Who gazed where, down that track of flame
A steamer to the west did dip:
Her heart went outward with the ship.

She had not kept her tryst that day,
Nor waved her hand to Allen Gray:
Both little hands were still — 'twas true
She could not "give her heart to two."

She heard the parting signals sound,
And then the haughty pride that bound
Her woman's heart, which had defied
Her woman's love, grew faint and died.

"She wandered hopeless to the strand,
And, hopeless, westward waved her hand."

She heard the steamship's iron bell;
Turned to the shore, but faltered, fell—
For ocean steamers do not wait
On love—her pride gave way too late.

"Too late!" she heard it rise and swell,
Tolled by the iron steamer's bell;
Told by the mocking voice of Fate,
Rung through her heart, "too late!" "too late!"

And now, when from that outward bound,
Defiant distance brought no sound,
She wandered hopeless to the strand,
And, hopeless, westward waved her hand.

The steamer's black smoke drifting far
Rose up and hid the evening star:
A bitter symbol of that strife
Between love's day-star and her life.

In the late gloaming's purple gloom
She wandered home; but half the bloom
Had faded from her cheek and lips:
Love's orient was in eclipse.

* * * * * * * * * * * *

* * * * * * * * * * * *

"The ship went down!" such message crossed
The lightning wire, and all were lost
Save Captain Gray, and two or three;
Among them was not Graham Lee.

From Daisy's hand the paper fell;
No cry she uttered, but a swell
Of anguish through her heart did sweep,
Bearing it downward to the deep.

As the green pallor of a storm
A summer landscape doth deform,
Making a livid shadow grow
Athwart the noon-day's ruddy glow,

Across the future once so fair,

So ripe with joy for Daisy Dare,

Fate's cruel sickle swept, and left

Life of its golden harvest reft.

"Turning her white cheek from the light,
Clasping her small hands fiercely tight!"

PART II.

WOMEN are deemed cold, careless, proud,
Who suffer bravely in a crowd;
Smiles flash from hearts in sorrow set,
As gleams from jewels edged with jet.

Some months had passed — it was not long —
When Daisy stood amid a throng,
Turning her white cheek from the light,
Clasping her small hands fiercely tight!

For she had heard two brave men say,—

A stranger one — one Allen Gray,—

No braver hero ever died

Than he whose love she lost through pride.

Unselfish, earnest, daring, brave,

All but himself he tried to save;

Heedless of death and danger — why?

One heart alone could make reply.

One spirit that had vainly sought

Rest from a hungry surge of thought;

Fierce retribution! — thus to be

Tortured by praise of Graham Lee!

Hero! but not for her to claim —
There was the anguish, there the shame:
How little yielding 'twould have cost
To call him still her own, though lost.

But she had cast away the right,
And, mutely wretched, heard that night,
With stormy heart and tearless cheek,
His praise whose name she dared not speak.

Few knew that they were lovers — none
That their two hearts had pulsed as one;
So the world called her cold and changed;
Friends thought her haughty and estranged.

The current of her life's May-time
Ran chill beneath a crust of rime;
And lovers wore, for Daisy's sake,
The icy chains they could not break.

A yearning sadness in her face
But added to that nameless grace,
That spell by which some women reign
In hearts they never strove to gain.

Love fell on her superb repose
Like warm light on a sculptured rose,
As if — beguiled — to flush apart
The chiselled whiteness of its heart.

DAISY DARE.

The voice of passion to her soul
Swept, as the storm-voiced surges roll
Up toward a star-like beacon steep,
Dashed backward rayless to the deep.

As fire-fly lighting up a maze
Of cobwebs with its dying blaze;
Held by a grim black spider fast —
Flashing with glory to the last.

Thus tangled in a cruel fate,
Dared through her folly, feared too late,
The light of Daisy's lost love made
The past fall back in deepest shade.

Strong natures suffer more than those
Who, bowing down, parade their woes
For a brief season, and then rise:
The brave heart uncomplaining dies.

So after years that inner gloom
Had only softened Daisy's bloom,
Giving such meaning to her eyes
As worldlings cannot analyze.

And when her pink cheek turned too soon
Pale as magnolia buds in June,
No one could call its fairness blight,
Or wish a flush upon the white.

When just one shade of roundness passed

From her proud form, they said at last

That she must travel. Well she knew

Love and regret would travel too!

'Twas not one shore alone, whose surge

Came wailing to her like a dirge;

The surf, the waves of every sea,

Everywhere, moaned of Graham Lee.

And when in a far distant land,

Upon a sunny southern strand,

Where warm waves, green as malachite,

Come leaping, as from vats of light,

Where summer's sumptuous golden blaze
Wraps earth in a voluptuous haze
Of lambent splendor; where the skies
Drop balm as erst in Paradise,

Where clusters of imperial trees
Nod their green plumes o'er slumberous seas;
Warm, amorous deeps! whose crystal calms
Dream of the emerald-crested palms.

A shore of bloom! a sea so bright!
Entranced they mingle in the light;
Apart — yet wedded by the sun,
As severed hearts through love made one.

Where air as an elixir fine
Exhilarates like sparkling wine;
Where mere existence brings a joy
Life's trifling ills cannot destroy:

There, where the aromatic breeze —
Fledged in a nest of orange-trees,
Kissing the slumb'rous waves — made sweet
The sea-foam swept to Daisy's feet.

The gloom, the shadow, passed not by;
Still white her cheek, as shells that lie
Like drifted snow on golden strand,
Where stood she writing in the sand.

And still the envious surges came
To wash away that precious name
Writ on her heart's warm shore for years,
Merged by its tidal flow of tears.

She stood in a sequestered cove,
While countless memories of love
Heaped treasure, till her sea of grief
Blushed — breaking on a coral-reef!

For precious memories often grow
From out the darkest voids of woe;
As fissures by the sea-worm drilled
In Eastern shells, with pearls are filled.

The creeping tide swells, shot with flame,
Stole up and kissed away that name
Which Fate indeed, with mocking hand,
For her had written in the sand.

Outward, upon her right did reach
A long, white, narrow line of beach,
Where careless groups now idly strayed,
Watching the flush of sunset fade.

And when across that crimson glow
Her gaze went out as long ago,
O'er colder seas, unto a ship
Which toward the setting sun did dip,

On the far point of that white sand
Standing together, hand in hand,
Like forms of sculptured bronze revealed
Against the sunset's burnished shield,

Two figures smote her 'wildered sight,
And left two blots upon the light;
Darker than iron ship afar
Or smoke that hid the evening star.

For there, between her and the sun,
Stood Graham Lee, and with him one
Whose beauty stirred to bitter strife
The chilly current of her life.

"Two figures smote her 'wildered sight,
And left two blots upon the light."

As summer sends a mighty thrill
Through clust'ring icy floes, until
Their shudd'ring breaks the ghastly sleep
Of Nova Zembla's pallid deep.

More dead he seemed to her that hour—
There, in the strength of manly power,
Bending to see those dark eyes shine—
Than cold and still beneath the brine.

Six years had marked their weary length
On her young life—whose faith and strength
A widowed heart left purified—
To live, now wishing she had died.

More lost she felt, and more alone,
Leaning against that hard, cold stone,
Than when his ship was outward bound,
Or when she thought of him as drowned.

They turned, and sauntered towards the cove;
Oh, woman's strength! oh, woman's love!
She stirred not till their eyes had met,
And knew herself remembered yet.

Down wastes of absence, grief, and gloom—
Warmed by his gaze—uprose the bloom
Of Hope's lost violets through the snow,
A purple path to long ago!

She saw the creole's large, dark eyes
Glance up to his in mute surprise;
She saw him leave the girl and stand
Before her with an outstretched hand.

Then turned and fled — no matter where,
So those she fled from were not there —
Seaward away, across the strand,
Where hungry waves crept up the sand.

On Memory's scroll there came a blot,
A space of time remembered not;
When sense awoke, clouds late aglow
With sunset fire, looked drifts of snow.

For, like a disembodied soul
By angels clad in silvery stole
And shining sandals for its flight
Along the upward paths of light,

The moon had risen there, and turned
Volcanic cloud-peaks while they burned,
White as the frozen coronet
On Jura's misty forehead set.

And where, from out her casket fine,
Eve had dropped rubies on the brine,
In gleaming lengths of shimmering sheen
Long lines of moonlight paved the green.

"Yet not to star, or sea, or skies
She gazed, but into deep, dear eyes."

Yet not to star, or sea, or skies
She gazed, but into deep, dear eyes
Bending upon her with the glow,
The old, sweet love of long ago.

Subtly it thrilled through every vein,
Making her white cheek flush again;
As pale hydrangeas blushing shine,
Whose roots are steeped in purple wine.

She felt love's subtle, potent charm
Binding her on that strong right arm;
'T was softer than the cold gray stone,
'T was sweeter thus than all alone.

One moment struggling to be free,

She cried: "Release me, Graham Lee;

For there is more to part us now

Than distance, death, or broken vow."

"Daisy"—his voice was deep and clear—

"Stay; would I dare to hold you here

So near my heart, if unto you

That heart had ever been untrue?

"Perchance, had I not found you soon,

As yon gray cloud beside the moon

Is silver-lined,—that wore a crown

Of glory when the sun went down,—

"My future might have worn at last
A light, which, likened to the past,
Would be as yonder placid moon
Unto the sumptuous suns of June.

"You thought me dead — I thought you lost;
Our hearts have both been tempest tossed,
And never anchored since that hour
When each defied the other's power.

"The stately creole by my side
Is my young sister — not my bride;
Earth holds one mate alone for me,
One bride — say, Daisy, shall it be?"

No blot on the horizon's verge,
No black smoke hid the star, no surge
Came up to fret the silent sea,
No answer came to Graham Lee.

What need of words? From eye to eye
How quick the magnet glances fly —
Electric sparks from soul to soul —
As magnets flash from pole to pole.

From noiseless waters, stealing slow,
The drooping white stalactites grow;
From noiseless drops stalagmites rise,
Silent they meet, and crystallize.

The overflowing loves that spring
From two proud natures meeting, cling
In strong, pure bliss from heart to home,
As cavern spars from floor to dome.

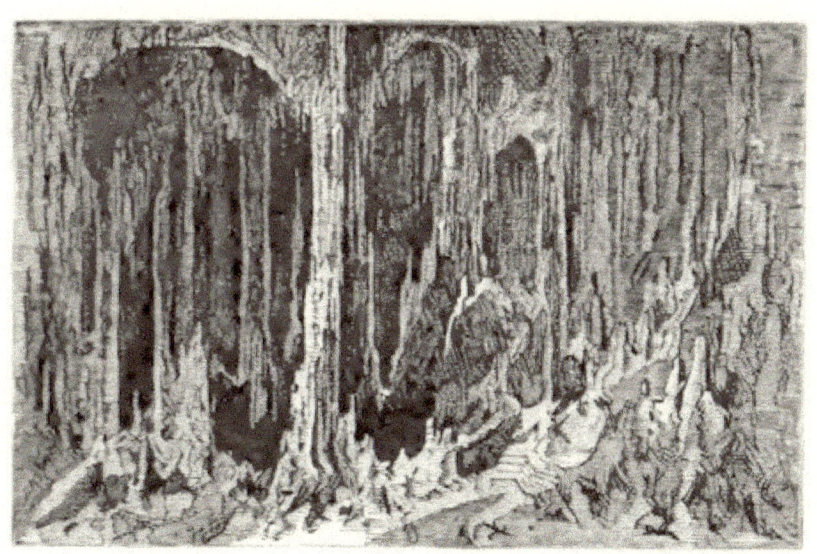

BABY POWER.

MULLEN,   PHOTO.

"Six little feet to cover,
Six little hands to fill,
Tumbling out in the clover,
Stumbling over the sill."

BABY POWER.

SIX little feet to cover,
    Six little hands to fill,
Tumbling out in the clover,
    Stumbling over the sill.
Six little stockings ripping,
    Six little shoes half worn;

Spite of the promised whipping,
 Skirts, shirts, and aprons torn!
Bugs and bumble-bees catching,
 Heedless of bites and stings,
Walls and furniture scratching,
 Twisting off buttons and strings.
Into the sugar and flour,
 Into the salt and meal,
Their royal, baby power,
 All through the house we feel!
Behind the big stove creeping,
 To steal the kindling-wood;
Into the cupboard peeping,
 To hunt for "somesin' dood."

The dogs they tease to snarling,
  The chickens know no rest,
Yet the old cook calls them "darling,"
  And loves each one "the best."
Smearing each other's faces
  With smut or blacking-brush,
To forbidden things and places
  Always making a rush.
Over a chair, or table,
  They'll fight, and kiss again
When told of slaughtered Abel,
  Or cruel, wicked Cain.
All sorts of mischief trying,
  On sunny days — in doors —

And then perversely crying
  To rush out when it pours.
A raid on grandma making,
  — In spite her nice new cap —
Its strings for bridles taking,
  While riding on her lap.
Three rose-bud mouths beguiling,
  Prattling the live-long day,
Six sweet eyes on me smiling,
  Hazel, and blue, and gray.—
Hazel — with heart-light sparkling,
  Too happy, we trust, to fade —
Blue — 'neath long lashes darkling,
  Like violets in the shade.

Gray — full of earnest meaning,
  A dawning light so fair,
Of woman's life beginning,
  We dread the noon-tide glare
Of earthly strife, and passion,
  May spoil its tender glow,
Change its celestial fashion,
  As earth-stains change the snow!
Six little clasped hands lifted,
  Three white brows upward turned,
One prayer — thrice heavenward drifted —
  To Him who never spurned
The lisp of lips where laughter,
  Fading away in prayer,

Leaves holy twilight after
    A noon of gladness there.
Three little heads, all sunny,
    To pillow and bless at night,—
Riotous Alick and Dunnie,
    Jinnie, so bonnie and bright!
Three souls immortal slumber,
    Crowned by that golden hair;
When Christ his flock shall number,
    Will all *my* lambs be there?
Now, with the stillness round me,
    I bow my head and pray,
"Since this faint heart has found thee,
    Suffer them not to stray."

BABY POWER.

Up to the shining portals,

Over life's stormy tide,

Treasures I bring — immortal;

Saviour be thou my guide.

www.ingramcontent.com/pod-product-compliance
Lightning Source LLC
Chambersburg PA
CBHW020244090426
42735CB00010B/1826